PRIZE
Awarded to

Rachel Hargrave

for

Conscientious Work

Date 11 · 7 · 84

PHILIP & TACEY LTD Andover Hants   Ref. 048-003-000

Growing up in
ELIZABETHAN
TIMES

Amanda Clarke

B.T. Batsford Ltd *London*

First published 1980
This edition published 1982

ISBN 0 7134 3364 7

Printed by R J Acford, Chichester, Sussex
for the Publishers B T Batsford Limited
4 Fitzhardinge Street, London W1H 0AH

Frontispiece **Two daughters of Lady Sidney**

Acknowledgment

The Author and Publishers thank the following
for their kind permission to reproduce copyright
illustrations: British Library for fig 32; the Trustees
of the British Museum for fig 2; the British Tourist
Authority for figs 22, 27, 49; Elizabeth Ewing
and Jean Webber for fig 29; Pat Hodgson Picture
Library for figs 16, 18, 19, 20, 39, 48, 56, 62;
A.F. Kerstring for fig 23; Mansell Collection for
fig 40; Museum of London for figs 6, 30, 35, 50;
National Maritime Museum for fig 34; National
Portrait Gallery for figs 8, 9, 28, 57, 63; Radio
Times Hulton Picture Library for figs 15, 21, 26,
31, 36, 37, 41, 45, 46, 47, 51, 52, 53, 54, 60, 61;
Victoria and Albert Museum for figs 1a, 1b, 7.
Thanks also are expressed to Pat Hodgson for the
picture research.

Contents

The Illustrations

1 The Elizabethan Age

The Elizabethan Age lasted from 1558 until 1603, and is considered by some to be "the most glorious and in some ways the most significant period of English history". Its influence and achievement were immense and its legacy is still being enjoyed today.

1a and b A tapestry of the English countryside, in about 1600. It shows the sheep, the hills and the dogs of which the foreign visitor England wrote (page 6). It looks a cheerful country.

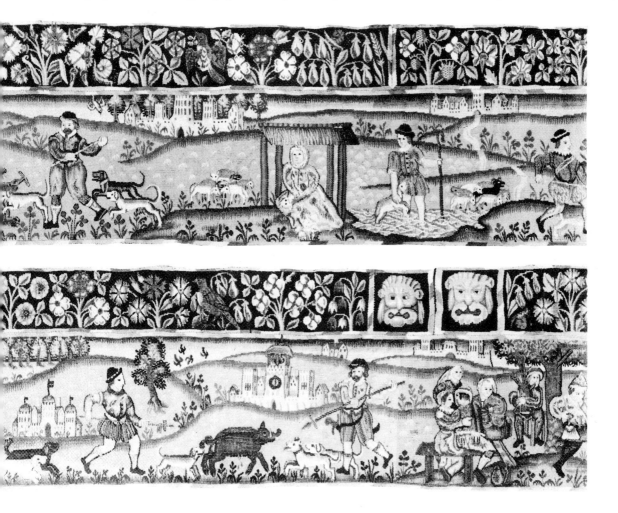

We have only to look at our houses, paintings and atlases to see that the Elizabethans are "alive and all around us", as the historian A.L. Rowse said.

The population of England at the end of Queen Elizabeth's reign was four million and four fifths of the people lived in the country. By modern standards, towns were small and well integrated into the countryside. London was the capital, and Norwich the second city.

A foreign visitor of 1598 described England:

The soil is fruitful and abounds with cattle . . . . The climate is temperate at all times . . . . The general drink is beer . . . and it is excellently well tasted, and strong and what soon fuddles . . . . There are many hills without one tree . . . upon these wander numerous flocks, extremely white . . . bearing softer and finer fleeces than those of any other country . . . . The dogs here are particularly good . . . . It has mines of gold, silver and tin. The horses are small but swift.

As for the English people, he considered them to be:

. . . grave . . . followed wherever they go by troops of servants . . . . They excel in dancing and music for they are lively and active . . . . They cut their hair close on the middle of their heads . . . . They are good sailors but better pirates . . . .

Loe here the pearle,
  whom God and man doth loue:
Loe here on earth,
  t he onely starre of light:
Loe here the Queene,
  whom no mishap can moue:
To chaunge her mynde,
  from vertues chief delight:

Loe here the heart,
  that so hath honord God:
That for her loue,
  we feele not of his rod:
Pray for her health,
  such as good subiectes bee:
(Oh Princely Dame,)
  there is none like to thee.

Hawking is a common sport of the gentry . . . . They are more polite in eating than the French, consuming less bread, but more meat. They put a great deal of sugar in their drink . . . . Their beds are covered with tapestry. . . . They are often molested with scurvy . . . . Their houses . . . are built of wood, the richer sort with bricks . . . . If they see a foreigner that is very well made, they will say "it is a pity that he is not an English Man."

During the Elizabethan period there was a dramatic rise in the population. It is estimated that between 1563 and 1603 the population of England and Wales rose by fifty per cent. This "explosion" was matched, and possibly caused by an improvement in the general standard of living. Although infant mortality was still very high, it was less than it would be in the seventeenth and eighteenth centuries. However, only one tenth of the population could hope to reach their fortieth birthday.

It was a time of extremes. The very rich could afford to live in magnificent

◄ **2   A woodcut portrait of Queen Elizabeth I, with a verse likening her to a precious pearl and star. The Queen was at the very top of the social ladder.**

3   An Elizabethan house built to an "E"-shape plan, the two wings forming the top and bottom strokes, and the entrance porch forming the centre of the "E". "E" was the Queen's initial.

houses and palaces, while the very poor existed in squalid huts or under hedges. The classes of society were clearly defined. Everyone was expected to know his place and to act accordingly. At the top of the social ladder was the Queen, around whom everything revolved. She was followed by the nobility, after which came the gentry, the yeomen, the labourers and lastly the wretched vagabonds. Movement from one class to another was difficult, but not impossible.

The Elizabethan Age has been nicknamed the time of the "Great Re-building". Beautiful new houses were built by anyone who could afford them, or else mediaeval houses were modernized to meet the new requirements. Chimneys and staircases were added, and glass was now at a price that most families could afford. Stone and brick were coming into fashion, replacing the traditional timber framing.

The Elizabethans were brimming over with curiosity and had a general thirst for

7

¶EVPHVES.

THE ANATOMY OF WYT.

Very pleafant for all Gentlemen to reade, and moſt nece/-
fary to remember:

wherin are contained the delights
that Wyt followeth in his youth by the
pleafauntneffe of Loue, and the
happyneffe he reapeth in
age, by
the perfectneffe of
Wifedome.

¶By Iohn Lylly Maſter of
Arte. Oxon,

¶Imprinted at London for
Gabriell Cawood, dwel-
ling in Paules Church-
yarde.

**4   The title page of *The Anatomy of Wit*.
St Paul's churchyard was the centre for book-
sellers.**

There was a major flowering of the arts. Music was considered extremely important and every one was expected to be able to play at least one musical instrument, and to sing reasonably well. Beautiful madrigals and plainsong were written by composers such as William Byrd and Thomas Tallis. Painting flourished, particularly portraits and miniatures by artists such as Nicholas Hilliard. The poetry of Edmund Spencer and Sir Walter Raleigh is still enjoyed today. And last, but far from least, the theatre blossomed in magnificent style. The Eliza-bethans Christopher Marlowe and William Shakespeare are two of the best playwrights England has ever produced.

Politically too, the Elizabethan Age was a time of experiment and exploration. The country was securely ruled by Queen Elizabeth I and her government. Through government machinery and an efficient Secret Service, the Privy Council were aware of everything that was happening in the kingdom. In Parliament, the House of Commons was slowly but surely emerging as a new vociferous element — a process which was to later result in the English Civil Wars 1642-48.

Throughout the reign of Elizabeth the

knowledge, no matter what the subject. Hundreds of books were published, and avidly read by men, women and children. Topics covered everything from how to make a knot garden (see page 37) to how to bring up children. The literacy rate was high and not achieved again until Victorian times. The explorers Hawkins, Frobisher and Drake discovered new lands and untold riches. Drake, in the *Golden Hind*, was the first man to circumnavigate the globe and English sea power was unquestioned after the English fleet had defeated the Spanish *Armada* in 1588.

8

5   A contemporary drawing of the Elizabethan poet Greene, who appears to be writing from right to left! Notice his writing equipment and the book which is fastened shut.

Church of England, established by Henry VIII, was strengthened. Through the Act of Supremacy the Queen was given the title of "Supreme Governor", and as such replaced the Pope as the head of the English church. This did not please everyone. Families which remained stubbornly Catholic found life increasingly difficult. Branded with the name "recusant", they were forced to worship in secret, or to pay heavy fines for not attending the Church of England services. Not all the Protestants were satisfied either. One group of them wanted to eliminate all traces of Catholicism from the Church of England. Because they wanted to "purify" it, they were nicknamed "Puritans".

All in all, the Elizabethan Age was an extremely exciting time to be alive.

6   This Delft plate showing the Tower of London expresses the excitement and confidence of the Elizabethan age.

2 Birth and Infancy

In Elizabethan times large families were common, and desperately wanted. It was not unusual to have as many as twelve or thirteen children, but it was rare for all of them to survive. Unhygienic conditions and lack of medical knowledge caused many children to die while they were still babies, and eight out of nine children died before they were five years old. Parents therefore had as many children as possible, hoping that some would survive to become adults.

The father was the head of the family — a family which could well include not only his children, but also elderly relatives, unmarried sisters and friends. It was his task to make sure that his children behaved properly, and that good marriages were arranged for them. The running of the household was left to the mother. She also looked after the children until they were seven, and educated her daughters.

Birth
As there were few reliable hospitals, a mother gave birth to her baby at home. She was helped by a midwife and her closest friends. The midwife had to promise not to exchange the new-born baby for a changeling (fairy child). Because pregnancy was often a difficult and dangerous time, the mother wore a charm round her neck to keep her from harm. Once labour began, the church bells were rung to frighten off all evil spirits. If it was a long birth, the midwife tied a piece of bell rope round the mother's waist, and loosened all the knots in the house — things like curtains and locks. When the baby was born, it was dressed in clothes that had belonged to its brothers and sisters, and a superstition said that it had to be carried upstairs before it went downstairs!

Baptism
As babies often died shortly after birth, they were usually baptized on the day they were born. The baptism was performed usually in the home, by the parish priest, and the ceremony was recorded in the parish register. The baby was dressed in a long, embroidered shirt for the baptism and afterwards was put in Chrism clothes, to show that it was now a Christian. After the baptism there was much feasting and drinking. Sometimes the father had a special cake baked, called the "Rocking Cake". Godparents and friends gave the baby presents such as Apostle spoons and coral necklaces, because they believed that "the coral preserveth such as weare it from fascination or bewitching". Babies were usually named after their parents or after members of the royal family. Elizabeth and Alice were popular names for girls, Thomas and John for boys. Some children were given more unusual names like Lettice and Cicely, Godshall and Mungham.

7   The brass of John Selwyn, showing his large family, in the church at Walton on Thames, Surrey. The words on the brass point out that John Selwyn's five sons and six daughters were all living when he died. It was unusual for all the babies born in a family to survive.

10

Babies' and infants' clothes

New-born babies were put into swaddling bands. A long strip of strong cloth was wound tightly round the baby's body, beginning at the armpits and going down to the hips. It was thought that this would keep the baby's spine straight and prevent it from breaking its legs by kicking. The tighter the swaddling clothes were pulled, the better it was believed to be for the child, and sometimes the baby's arms were bound too.

Some babies were not only swaddled, but had to wear other clothes on top! In an imaginary conversation, written in 1568, a mother says to the nurse:

> How now, how doeth the child . . . unswaddle him, undo his swaddling bands . . . wash him before me . . . . Pull off his shirt . . . now swaddle him again, but first put on his biggin [a little cap] and his little band [collar] with an edge, where is his little petticoat? Give him his coat of Changeable [shot] taffetta and his satin sleeves; where is his bib? Let him have his gathered apron strings and hang a muckinder [long handkerchief] to it. You need not yet give him

his coral with the small gold chain, for I believe it is better to let him sleep until the afternoon . . . . God send thee sound rest my little boykin.

8 **An Elizabethan mother and baby. The nurse looks on. Notice the rocking cradle and the pet dog. (From the portrait of Sir Henry Unton).**

Quite a formidable array for a small baby!

Royal children were even worse off. When Queen Elizabeth was only three years old, her nurse wrote a letter to the Lord Chancellor:

beseeching . . . that she may have some raiment . . . for she [Elizabeth] hath neither gown, nor kirtle, nor petticoat,

nor no manner of linen, nor fore smock [pinafore], nor kerchiefs, nor rails [nightgowns], nor body stitchet [corset], nor handkerchiefs, nor sleeves, nor mufflers [day cap], nor biggin . . .

Little boys wore long skirts and petticoats like their sisters' until they were six or seven years old. Then they were ceremoniously "breeched": their first pair of breeches was put on, and they became "men".

9 Sir Walter Raleigh, the explorer, and his son, who has been "breeched". He stands in the same pose as his father and looks a real man.

Feeding

Some babies were sent out to a wet nurse to be fed. This woman was carefully chosen, for people believed that the baby sucked in the character of the wet nurse along with her milk. An Elizabethan called Thomas Phayre advised parents not to choose a wet nurse who was "a drunkard, vicious, sluttish or such that corrupteth the nature of the child". Wet nurses were becoming unfashionable and many mothers began feeding their babies themselves. There were no special baby foods, and so babies were not weaned until they were between two and four years old. Cows' horns were sometimes used as feeding bottles.

Nurseries

If the parents were wealthy enough, they employed a nurse to look after their baby. She and her charges were kept securely in the nursery. The contents of one nursery in 1567 were "one trundle bed, with a feather bed, a mattress, blankets, sheets, coverlets, with a covering and a bolster; one chest, a presser [cupboard with hanging space] with a chair . . .". Tiny babies slept in wooden cradles on rockers, while older children all slept together in one big bed. The famous Great Bed of Ware in the Victoria and Albert Museum, was meant to sleep twelve people.

To help them to learn to walk, children had reins attached to their clothes, called "hanging sleeves", and wooden cages on wheels which were attached to their waists.

Elizabethan children had many of the toys we know today, from rattles and teething rings to popguns and drums. Dolls, made out of wood or material, were bought at fairs and markets. They were nicknamed "Bartholomew babies" after Bartholomew Fair, the most famous of all. Many of the nursery rhymes sung by Elizabethan children are still sung today. Favourites included "Hush a Bye Baby", "Three Blind Mice" and "The Frog he would a Wooing Go".

14

Old Mother Hubbard, Little Jack Horner and Tom Thumb were familiar nursery characters.

Manners and discipline

Elizabethan parents were very strict. They needed to be with such large families. Parents were addressed as "sir" and "madam", and they expected good behaviour at all times. There were many books available to tell parents how to bring up their children properly. *The Boke of Nurture, or Schole of Good Manners* by Hugh Rhodes gave the following advice to fathers:

> to cause their children . . . to use fair and gentle speech . . . with reverence and courtesy to their elders . . . . Apparel not your children in sumptuous apparel . . . nor let your children go whither they will, but know where they go . . . and when you hear them swear or curse, lie or fight, thou shalt sharply reprove them.

He also warned children not to speak with

10   The child in the front is taking its first steps aided by the wooden cage on wheels. The boy has a hobby horse, not much different from those of today.

their mouths full, nor to scratch their heads when they were eating, nor to spit on the table!

Church

Religion played a very large part in every family's life, no matter what branch of Christianity they believed in. The entire family was expected to go to church every Sunday. If they did not, they were liable to pay a minimum fine of one shilling (5p) each. Many people were sad that since the Reformation and the founding of the Church of England their once ornate, colourful and perfumed churches had been stripped of their decoration. The statues of saints had been destroyed as being idolatrous, and the elaborate church furnishings had been banned. Even so, Elizabethan churches were colourful by modern standards. The walls were not just whitewashed, but were adorned with paintings telling stories from the Bible and with simple flower patterns. Tombs were also gaily painted.

Services were held according to the Prayer Book issued in 1552, with one or two amendments from the 1554 version. A typical day's services were Matins at 7.00 a.m., Communion during the morning, and Vespers at 2.00 p.m. The services like the buildings were much simpler and plainer than before the Reformation. One man sighed:

Alas . . . what shall we do now at church, since all the saints are taken away; since all the goodly sights we were wont to have are gone; since we cannot hear the piping, singing, chanting, and playing upon the organ, that we could before?

Another mournfully declared: "there is blue ice in our churches."

This is rather a gloomy picture for, compared with our bare but dignified churches, Elizabethan ones were bustling with life — as was the congregation:

They are a kind of people that love a pot of ale better than a pulpit, and a corn rick better than a church door, who, coming to divine service more for fashion than devotion, are contented after a little capping and kneeling, coughing and spitting, to help me [the parson] sing out a psalm and sleep at the second lesson, or awake to stand up at the gospel, and say "Amen" at the peace of God, and stay till the banns of matrimony be called . . . and then . . . be glad to be gotten home to dinner.

11   A family meal.

THE BIBLE
AND
HOLY SCRIPTVRES
CONTEYNED IN
THE OLDE AND NEWE
Testament.

TRANSLATED ACCOR-
*ding to the Ebrue and Greke, and conferred with
the best tranflations in diuers langages.*

WITH MOSTE PROFITABLE ANNOTA-
tions vpon all the hard places, and other things of great
importance as may appeare in the Epiftle to the Reader.

FEARE YE NOT, STAND STIL, AND BEHOLDE
the faluacion of the Lord, which he wil fhewe to you this day. Exod. 14, 13.

THE LORD SHAL FIGHT FOR YOU: THEREFORE
holde you your peace, Exod. 14, vers. 14.

AT GENEVA.
PRINTED BY ROULAND HALL.

MDLX.

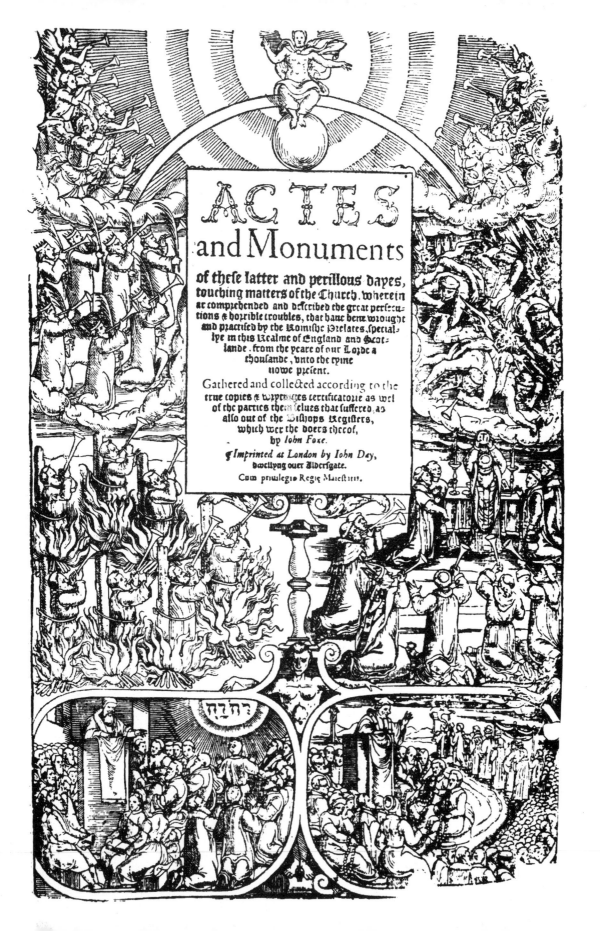

ACTES
and Monuments

of these latter and perillous dayes,
touching matters of the Church. wherein
ar comprehended and described the great persecu-
tions & horrible troubles, that haue been wrought
and practised by the Romishe Prelates, special-
lye in this Realme of England and Scot-
lande, from the yeare of our Lorde a
thousande, vnto the tyme
nowe present.

Gathered and collected according to the
true copies & wrytynges certificatorie as wel
of the parties them selues that suffered, as
also out of the Bishops Registers,
which wer the doers thereof,
by Iohn Foxe.

¶ Imprinted at London by Iohn Day,
dwellyng ouer Aldersgate.
Cum priuilegio Regię Maiestatis.

Religion at home

Almost every family, no matter how poor, possessed at least two books: the Bible — which was translated into English and made into a portable size in 1579 — and Foxe's *Actes and Monuments*, or *Book of Martyrs* as it is better known. Now that the Bible was available to literally everyone who could read or listen, reading the Bible became a favourite family pastime. Families clustered round the father as he read out passages and explained the meanings of the stories. Children had to learn large chunks of the Bible by heart and were expected to hold theological conversations with their parents and teachers. Sometimes children read the Bible to their parents while they were eating a meal!

Foxe's *Book of Martyrs*, first published in English in 1564, went into five editions during Elizabeth's reign. It was placed in every public place, including cathedrals, Bishops' palaces, orphanages, and in the homes of the gentry and nobility, so that everyone could read it whenever they wished. It contained a list of all Protestant martyrs, an outline of ecclesiastical history and the interesting theory that the English were God's chosen people. This, of course, went down very well, and merely reinforced what the Elizabethans had already realized!

Catholic families

Acts were passed forbidding the celebration of mass, the main Catholic service, and so Catholics had to worship in secret. As already mentioned, everyone was expected to go to church, and Catholics were no exception. They were often forced to attend a Church of England service, and then went home to hold a secret mass. This was a dangerous practice, for if they were discovered the penalties were severe. To be a Catholic priest was a crime punishable by death (see picture 44), while families faced crippling fines. In spite of this many families did remain Catholic. In the late 1570s and early 1580s Jesuit priests arrived in England and attempted to reassure and reconvert the Catholics. Again their work had to be done in secret.

Puritans

The Puritans, who wanted to "purify" the Church of England by having simpler services and less ceremony, were also treated unsympathetically. Elizabeth saw them as a threat to her authority and treated them in much the same way as the Catholics. Puritan families were fined by their parish if they did not go to church, and Puritans were forbidden to preach.

Pledgings

Some children were pledged to be married when they were still only infants. This meant that they promised to marry someone chosen by their parents, when they were old enough. One little three-year-old called Robert Barre was so upset at his pledging that he had to be "lured for an apple by his uncle to go to the church". A few child marriages did take place, but these were rare and the children returned to live with their parents until they were old enough to be married properly.

3 Country Children

Four fifths of the population lived in the countryside. Imagine the huge stretches of woodland and fields, with no telegraph poles, cars or sky-scrapers to spoil the view. Life may have been more peaceful — but it certainly was not easier. Farming was the main activity. Men who owned their own farms were called yeomen or husbandmen. They were usually able to live comfortably. Tenant farmers rented land to work on, while labourers owned no land and were hired hands. Life on the farm was ruled by the seasons and the weather, and everyone, including the children, had to work. There were no tractors and combine harvesters to do the heavy work. Everything had to be done by hand, with the aid of primitive implements and animals such as horses and oxen. Rye, wheat and barley were the main crops, and at harvest time every capable body was required to help get in all the grain before the weather broke. The threat of a bad harvest and starvation was never far away.

Homes

Yeomen lived in timber-framed cottages, which had wattle and daub walls (woven willow sticks filled in with mud and dung) and thatched roofs. Wealthy yeomen began to add chimneys and staircases to their mediaeval homes, and to roof in the huge hall to make an upper storey.

14 A yeoman speaks to an ordinary peasant woman.

Poorer farmers continued to live in primitive conditions. Their houses were only one storey high and were cruck cottages. Some lived in cob cottages, which had no timber frame but were made out of mud, lime and straw which hardened into a solid wall. Inside they were dark, smokey and smelly. The floor was beaten earth covered with rushes or hay. The rushes were not changed very often, and so "an ancient collection of beer and grease, fragment of fish and everything nasty" congealed there.

15 Hard and hot work at harvest time. The last sheaf of corn would be dressed up as the Harvest Queen.

Furniture

Homes were sparsely furnished but the furniture was solidly built. Rich yeomen and their families slept in truckle beds, but many people just lay on a straw pallet and covered themselves with a blanket when they wanted to go to sleep. Although some people used pillows, these were still unfashionable in the country, most people preferring to use logs! There were solid oak tables to eat from, cupboards and chests to keep valuables in, stools and benches, but very few chairs. Conditions cannot have been too bad, judging from this rosy picture painted by an Elizabethan called Harrison:

> many farmers . . . have for the most part learned also to garnish cupboard with plate, their joined beds with tapestry and silk hangings, and their tables with carpets and fine napery.

Food

Good ploughman took weekly of custom and right
For roast meat on Sunday, Thursday and night.

Farmers and their families ate three meals a day. Breakfast was eaten between six and seven o'clock in the morning and consisted of bread, cheese, porridge and ale. The other meals were taken at midday and at six in the evening. The midday meal was bread and cheese, but meat and vegetable stews formed the main evening meal. Honey was used as a sweetener instead of sugar, which was still very expensive. Most families kept their own bees, housed in neat little wicker-work hives. Food was eaten either off large hunks of bread called trenchers, or from wooden plates. Ale was the main drink, enjoyed by everyone including children. Housewives brewed the ale at home and if they wanted to sell it too, they had merely to hang a bush over the door and the house became an instant off-licence.

Clothes

Country clothes had to be more practical and hard-wearing than those worn by townspeople. By order of an Act of Parliament, labourers were meant to wear brown, blue or tawny-coloured clothes. However, some farmers were very fashion-conscious, as one Elizabethan remarked:

> The ploughman, that in times past was content in russet, hath nowadays must his doublet of the fashion, with wide cuts, his garters of fine silk.

Boys wore a shirt and a fitted jacket called a doublet. Instead of trousers they had knee-length breeches and tight-fitting hose. Girls wore long skirts and separate bodices. During Elizabeth's reign a law was passed which said that all humble-born females were to wear at least one woollen petticoat. This was to help the wool trade! This poem written in 1575, describes a country girl's wardrobe:

> *Two fair new kirtles on her back,*
> *The one was blue, the other black.*
> *For Holy-days she had a gown*
> *And every yard did cost a crown*

16   Inside a country cottage. It is smokey and there is little furniture. Another young child is learning to walk in a wheeled cage.

And more by eighteen pence I guess.
She had three smocks, she had no less
Four rails and eke five handkerchiefs fair
Of hose and shoes she had a pair
She needed not no more to have,
She would go barefoot for to save
Her shoes and hose, for they were dear.

Only rich children could afford to sleep in long, white nightgowns. Country children slept in their day shirts, but they might have had a bright red nightcap!

Cleanliness

Frequent baths were not considered necessary. About once a month a large tub was filled with water and placed in front of the fire for a bath, or else a visit was made to the nearest river. Soap was made out of ashes and animal fats, scented with herbs and flowers. Teeth were cleaned with a peculiar mouthwash made out of "dragon's herb, boll armanack, allum, honey, cinnamon, and spring water". Toothpicks were used extensively.

As for lavatories, some private homes had houses of easement but most people preferred to nip behind the nearest tree. In 1597 Sir John Harrington invented the first water-closet. Although the Queen had one installed in Richmond Palace, no-one else seems to have been impressed.

Boys' work

As soon as they were strong enough, boys were expected to help their fathers on the land. They helped with the ploughing, sowing and harvesting. In the autumn they collected acorns to feed the pigs, or gathered honey from the hives. Very small boys were "armed with string or with bow, to scare away pigeon, the rook and the crow".

17 The difference between a courtier's clothing and a country man's clothing: "velvet breeches and cloth breeches".

18   A wicker-work beehive.

19   Public washing grounds, on the banks of a stream, 1582. The women had to pound the washing in the tubs or actually wash it in the stream.

Girls' work

Girls were taught by their mothers how to be competent housewives. The number of skills they had to learn was enormous. This is one farmer's description of how a good wife should behave: she should

> pray when first getting out of bed, then clean the house, dress the dishboard, milk the cows, suckle the calves, dress her children, cook meals for the household, brew and bake when needed, send corn to the mill, make butter and cheese, look after the swine and collect the eggs.

Girls also had to collect down for the mattresses, help with the three-monthly linen washing, make candles, spin, weave and embroider pretty things for their bottom drawer.

20   Christmas festivities. The Yule-log is dragged ▶ inside.

24

Militia

In time of war every village was expected to provide as many able-bodied men and boys to fight as possible. These little village groups combined to form the national militia, which was mustered by the Lord Lieutenants of the counties during times of impending war. Each village boy spent a lot of time training for these musters. He learnt how to fight and how to handle a bow and arrow. One Elizabethan proudly remarked:

> there is almost no village, be it never so small, that hath not sufficient arms in readiness to send forth three or four men in times of war.

Country customs

Country people celebrated many ancient customs, some of which have come down to us today. The most well-known celebration was May Day, when the maypole "sometimes painted with variable colours" was put up on the village green, where the villagers danced about it "like the heathen people did". After the harvest the last sheaf of corn was dressed up as a girl in actual clothes and called the Harvest Queen. It was kept in a safe place — often in the tithe barn or the church — until the next year when a new Harvest Queen was made. At Hallowe'en

bonfires were lit and villagers wore masks to prevent the evil spirits from recognizing them. On Shrove Tuesday people made pancakes to eat, and a special Pancake Bell was rung. Hot cross buns were made at Easter, but they were not eaten — they were saved as charms instead. On All Saints' Day the dead were believed to return to their former homes, and so bonfires were lit to show them the way.

Christmas

This was the most important festival of the year and an occasion for twelve days of feasting, drinking and playing. On Christmas Eve every village chose a Lord of the Misrule to be in charge of the entertainment. He chose

> twenty, forty, a hundred lusty lads like himself, decketh them in his liveries of green, yellow and some light colour. They bedeck themselves with scarves, ribbons, and laces, hanged all over with gold rings and jewels.

These men were then responsible for organizing all the festivities. On Christmas Day there was a huge feast when a pie made out of neat's (oxen's) tongues, chickens, eggs, sugar, raisins and spices was eaten. Presents were usually saved until New Year's Day.

25

4 Noble Children

A small proportion of the population was made up of two envied and privileged classes — the nobility and the gentry, rich and important people, whose lives were enormously different from those of the merchant, yeomen and pauper families. The nobility were a high-born group of people, often related to the royal family.

Their children were sent to Court as attendants to the Queen. The gentry were well-born country people, with great influence in their home counties. They were knights

21 A nobleman, a merchant and a gentleman — men from three different classes of Elizabethan society.

22 Little Moreton Hall, a gentry home.

23 Hardwick Hall, with its enormous windows. The fashion was to have "more glass than wall".

as opposed to lords.

Children of these families lived in large, impressive buildings, for

no sooner doth a man succeedeth in the sixteenth century than he builde himself a new home and more than one if he could afford it.

Many of these richer Elizabethan houses still exist today. Good examples of gentry homes are Little Moreton Hall and Adlington Hall in Cheshire, while Hardwick Hall and Longleat are rather grander.

Children of the privileged classes were beautifully, if not strangely dressed, well fed and well disciplined. They had servants and nurses to attend them, tutors to teach them and a wealth of amusements.

Homes

Houses were large and elaborate, and a good means of showing off to neighbours. In the Elizabethan period old houses were mod-

ernized and new houses built such as had never been seen before. New houses were often built to an "E"-shaped plan (supposedly using the Queen's initial — see picture 4). The entrance hall made the middle stroke of the "E" and the wings of the house formed the top and bottom strokes. Huge, decorated front doors and large windows were popular. Lord Bacon remarked:

> You should have sometimes fair houses, so full of glass that one cannot tell where to come to be out of the sun or cold.

Hardwick Hall achieved this "more glass than wall" fashion most splendidly.

◄ 24 Elizabethan oak cupboard.

The great houses and the more humble manor houses were to a large extent self-sufficient. As well as the usual rooms such as bedrooms and kitchens, they also had bakehouses, dairies, butteries, pantries and breweries where all the food preparation and storage went on.

Furniture

We might find the interiors of these rich houses sparsely furnished, cold and dark compared to our own modern homes. Furniture was solid and heavy, ornately

carved with figures and flowers. There were chests, tables, stools, cupboards, wardrobes and a few chairs. The most important item of furniture was the bed. This was a four-poster which was panelled and carved, and had a wooden canopy (tester) from which hung heavy, embroidered curtains. Beds were so valuable that they were handed down from generation to generation.

Rushes were the most usual floor covering, although some families were taking their Turkish carpets off the walls and putting them on the floors. There was no wallpaper, but beautiful, hand-sewn tapestries on the walls kept out the draughts. Sometimes walls were panelled with oak, or painted with flowers and stories from the Bible.

26   An Elizabethan kitchen. The meat is cooked on spits.

**27   This Elizabethan kitchen at Halls Croft,   ►
Stratford, can be visited today. Notice the bellows hanging by the fireplace, which were used to keep the fire going. Imagine the sort of activity shown in picture 26 going on in this room.**

Food

Meals were sumptuous and lengthy, far removed from the bread and cheese of the yeoman's table. The main meal was eaten at 11.00 a.m. and could last as long as three hours. Meals were eaten in the dining-parlour, though children sometimes ate in the nursery. Meat, cheese and bread were eaten in abundance, but were far more varied than poor people's food. Noble children ate fine white bread, instead of the course rye bread eaten in the country. Meat was not limited to mutton or beef, but included such delicacies as plover, pheasant, peacock, swan and blackbird. In 1572 one dozen blackbirds cost one shilling, and six shillings bought a cygnet. The Elizabethans had no refrigerators or freezers and often unfresh meat had to be eaten. It was heavily spiced and herbed to disguise the taste. If the meat went "green", cooks were advised to wrap it up in a cloth and bury it for twelve to twenty hours, after which time it would be all right for consumption. Most big houses had their own fishponds, and until 1585 it was compulsory to eat fish on every Wednesday and Friday. Cheeses were enjoyed, and rancid butter was considered good for the digestion. Potatoes were known after 1564 but were not very popular. Elizabethan children loved sweet things, but only wealthy parents could

afford to pay 4s 10d a pound for sugar. Custards, marchpanes (marzipan), syllabubs, crystallized fruits, gingerbread and kissing comfits (to sweeten the breath) were all eaten in vast quantities. It is not surprising to hear that many Elizabethans suffered from black, rotten teeth.

Drink

Twenty to thirty tons of wine were imported into England each year, but only the rich could afford to drink it. Wine was often spiced, watered down or sweetened. A recipe for a strange mixture called "Ypocras" said: "mix cinnamon, ginger, nutmeg, cloves and pepper and steep in white wine for six days", after which time it was ready to drink. Ale, mead, perry and cider were also enjoyed by everyone, including children. In 1588 three pints of cider cost 4d, while a small barrel of beer cost 4s 4d.

Kitchens

It is not surprising that kitchens had to be large and carefully designed. They contained several ovens and open hearths, with roasting spits and all manner of utensils. Herbs, coal, pots and pans were kept in the "Squillerie" (scullery), while different foods were put in to either the wet or the dry larder. It must have been very hot and tiring working in such conditions. Kitchens were sometimes built outside the house, or on the opposite wing to the dining-parlour, and so food was frequently cool by the time it reached the family and their guests at table.

Girls' clothes

Children wore miniature versions of their parents' clothes, and judging by the portraits (pictures 9, 28, 31), they were not very comfortable. Can you imagine going out to play in some of these clothes? In the morning a noble girl first put on her chemise, which was like a long, white nightdress. Next came some woollen stockings, which were held up with garters tied at the knee. She put on a corset, made out of leather or stiffened material, which tied down the front. Over this, she put on a separate bodice, followed by sleeves which were attached by strings under her arms. Then she put on her farthingale. This odd-looking garment was a kind of petticoat. Hoops in the petticoat, made out of whalebone,

formed a frame over which the girl's skirt would stick out. Several layers of petticoats were put on over the farthingale. The top one, called a "kirtle", was embroidered and allowed to show through the central opening of her overskirt. Finally, the girl put on a stomacher over her bodice. This was like another stiff corset, which came down to a point just below her waist. Not everyone thought such restricting garments were healthy, and one father wrote about the effects they had had on his daughter:

> I had the advice of an able physician . . . his judgment was that her bodice was her pain and hindered her lungs to grow, and truth the surgeon found her breast bone pressed very deeply inwards and he said two of her ribs were broken.

The little girl in question was only two years old.

Gowns were lavishly embroidered and made of "silk . . . velvet . . . grosgrain . . . taffeta", and there were such delightful colours as Popinjay Blue, Pease Pudding Tawny, Judas Colour, and even Goose Turd Green to choose from. Ruffs, made out of starched or wired lawn, were worn at the neck, and every imaginable kind of jewellery was fashionable. Not everyone approved of the final result, as one man remarked:

> When they [girls] have all these goodly robes upon them they seem to be . . . not . . . women of flesh and blood . . . but rather puppets.

Beauty

To be considered beautiful, an Elizabethan girl had to have extremely white skin, blue eyes, ruby lips and fair hair. Those unfortunate enough to have been born without these requirements had to cheat — using very peculiar, and dangerous methods. Dark hair was bleached with sulphur and lead, which eventually made it fall out. This didn't really matter, for "they [girls] are not simply content with their own hair, but buy other hair either of horse, mare or

28 Lady Sidney and six of her children, all dressed in miniature versions of their mother's clothes.

29 A farthingale. This petticoat, with its whalebone hoops, was a frame for the girl's skirts.

30   A selection of sixteenth-century jewellery.

any other strange beast". To get the desirable white face, a deadly mixture of lead and vinegar was plastered on, which tended to have the same results as mummification. Lipstick was made out of cochineal and egg whites, while poisonous belladonna (a drug made from deadly nightshade) was dropped into the eyes to make them look larger. Mothers were advised to bathe their children in milk to give them pale skins; and freckles, which were considered ugly, were treated with brimstone. Perfumes were very popular — mainly to hide the many other nasty smells.

Boys' clothes

Boys were also subjected to the discomfort of stiff, ungainly clothes. In 1585 one man described typical male costume:

> They have great and monstrous ruffs . . . their doublets are no less monstrous than the rest, for now the fashion is to let them down to the middle of their thighs . . . being so hard quilted, stuffed, bombasted . . . as they can neither work, nor yet well play in them, through the excess heat thereof . . . they have cloaks also . . . of divers colours.

Doublets were made out of "satin, taffeta, silk, gold, silver, slashed, fagged, cut, carved, pinked and laced". Hats were "fantastic",

34

31 This boy has no ruff, but his clothes look stiff and heavy and difficult to play in.

and in 1571 an Act was passed which said that every male over the age of seven was to wear a cap made of "woolknit, thicked and dressed" — again to help the ailing wool trade (see page 21). For those able to grow them, moustaches were "fostered about the ears like branches of a vine".

Boys

Boys were expected to act like miniature adults at all times. "He's like a man" was the biggest compliment paid to a boy, no matter how young. Discipline was very strict and there was no time for silly behaviour. At the age of seven some boys were sent away to other noble households to become pages. This meant that they became the personal servants of the master of the house, who, in return, taught them all the social graces expected of a young nobleman. One Italian visitor was shocked by this custom and wrote

> The want in affection in England is strongly manifested towards their children, for having kept them at home till they arrive at the age of seven or nine years . . . they put them out . . . to hand service in the houses of other people . . . and on inquiring the reason for this severity they answered that they did it that their children might learn better manners.

Girls were often sent out for the same reasons.

Girls

Like yeomen children, the daughters of noblemen were taught by their mothers how to become good housewives. They had to learn to supervise servants, prepare exotic menus and organize the running of a large household. They also had to be skilled in dancing, singing and embroidery. To perfect their sewing, they worked on samplers. These were long strips of linen

on which they practised their stitches.
A girl was expected to be

> of chaste thought, stout courage, patient,
> untiring, watchful, diligent, witty, pleas-
> ant, constant in friendship, full of good
> neighbourhood, wise in discourse . . .
> secret in her affairs. . . and generally
> skilful in all worldly knowledge which
> do belong to her vocation.

Marriage

Like country and town children, noble
children had their marriages arranged for
them by their parents. Marriage was very
desirable, especially for girls for whom there
were no alternative careers. Few wanted to
stay at home, contenting themselves with
spinning (hence the word "spinster"). Noble
children generally got married slightly

younger than country children, but again child marriages were the exception rather than the rule.

Once married, Elizabethan girls do not appear to have been meek or nondescript wives. Thomas Platter noted that

the womenfolk of England, who have mostly blue-grey eyes and are fair and pretty, have far more liberty than in any other land . . . and the men must put up with such ways, and may not punish them for it, indeed the good wives often beat their men.

Gardens

The Elizabethans were very fond of gardens, and every noble family had a magnificent, well-stocked one. Sir Francis Bacon believed that "God Almighty first planted a garden, indeed it is the purest of human pleasures." There were many books available on the subject, such as Thomas Hill's *Profitable Art of Gardening*, first published in 1563. Gardens were carefully planned and formally laid out. Lawns, mazes and shrubs were arranged in elaborate knot patterns. The herb garden was essential, both for cooking and medical purposes. Mint, hyssop, chervil, tarragon and parsley were popular. Favourite flowers included pansies, hollyhocks, poppies and snapdragons.

◄ **32**   A design for a knot garden. The shrubs would be planted out in this pattern.

33   This formally laid out garden is being watered by means of pumps in a tub of water. Notice the beehives in the right-hand corner.
▼

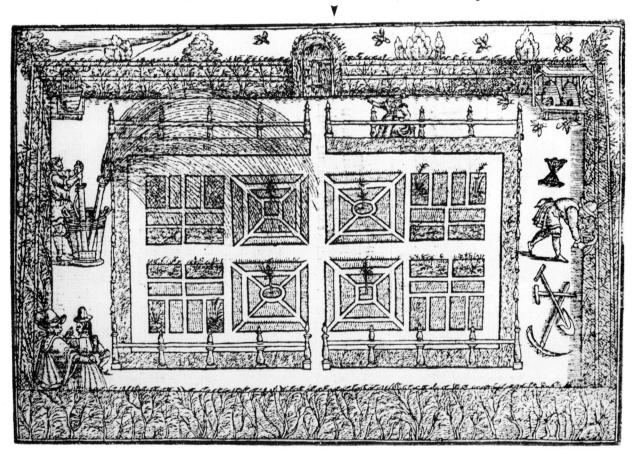

5 Town Children

One fifth of the population lived in towns but, by modern standards, Elizabethan towns were little more than villages, in both size and appearance. London, the "noblest town of the noblest nation", had a population of 60,000; Norwich had 12,000, Bristol 10,000, Exeter 8,000, York 7,500 and Coventry 6,600. There was no heavy industry, and so towns had a rural air, with trees, gardens and open spaces. Most towns were still surrounded by their mediaeval walls and inside was a strange mixture of dingy slums

34 Bristol in about 1590. The medieval wall still stands. People in the town could quickly reach the open country.

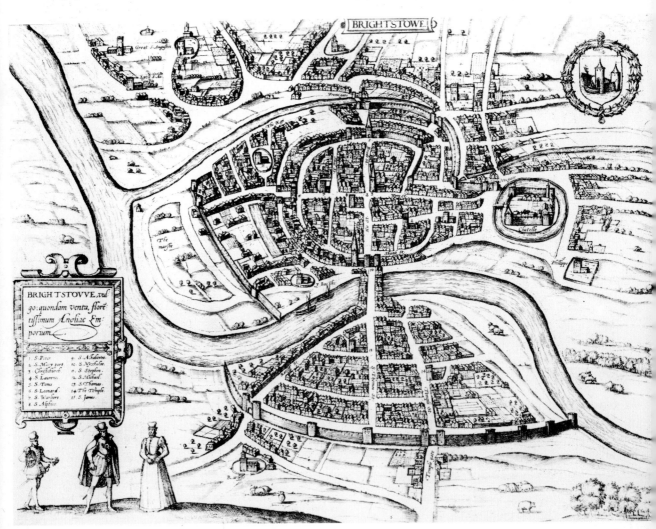

35   A model of the Royal Exchange, London, in the sixteenth century. The model gives an impression of the village-like air of the town, but it does not give any idea of the busy-ness of the narrow streets.

and beautiful merchant houses; interesting shops and appalling filth; elegant gentry and flea-ridden beggars.

Many things about Elizabethan towns would surprise us. We would be astounded by the smell. Although men called "scavengers" were employed to collect the rubbish, they did not do the job very well. Consequently, the narrow streets were piled high with refuse, sewage, dead dogs, rotting vegetables and general litter. Instead of removing the cause of the smell, the Eliza-bethans carried pomanders or herbs about with them which they could hold to their noses to blot out the other smells. Pomanders were made out of fresh oranges stuck with cloves, which were then dried and worn hanging from the waist. People also carried sweet herbs in little silver containers round their neck or in linen bags.

The colourful clothes would surprise us. Everyone, including men and boys, loved to dress in cheerful-coloured clothes, the more colours worn the better.

And we would notice the different noises of an Elizabethan town. No road drills, car hooters or motor-bikes, but the rumbling of carts, clatter of hooves and shouts of the street sellers. As one man wrote, "In every street, carts and coaches

36 A crowd of people have come to see a woman being ducked. Punishments always attracted spectators.

make such a thundering as if the world ran upon wheels". Though small, towns were bustling with people, all eager to lead their lives to the full:

At every corner men, women and children meet in shoals . . . here are porters sweating under their burdens, the merchantmen breathing bags of money, chapmen. . . skip out of one shop into another . . . tradesmen are busy and never stand still.

London was even more lively and was not only "brimful of curiosity but so populous that one simply cannot walk along the streets for the crowd", especially when there was a slaughtering or a hanging.

Houses

Most town houses dated from mediaeval times, and had been built higgledy-piggledy. Some houses had as many as five storeys, each one projecting over the one below, so that the top floors of houses opposite each other nearly met across the street. This made the street below dark, sinister and airless. Houses were timber-framed, with wattle and daub walls covered with plaster. Sometimes the beams were ornately carved or the plaster was moulded into patterns (pargeting). Poorer families lived in slum

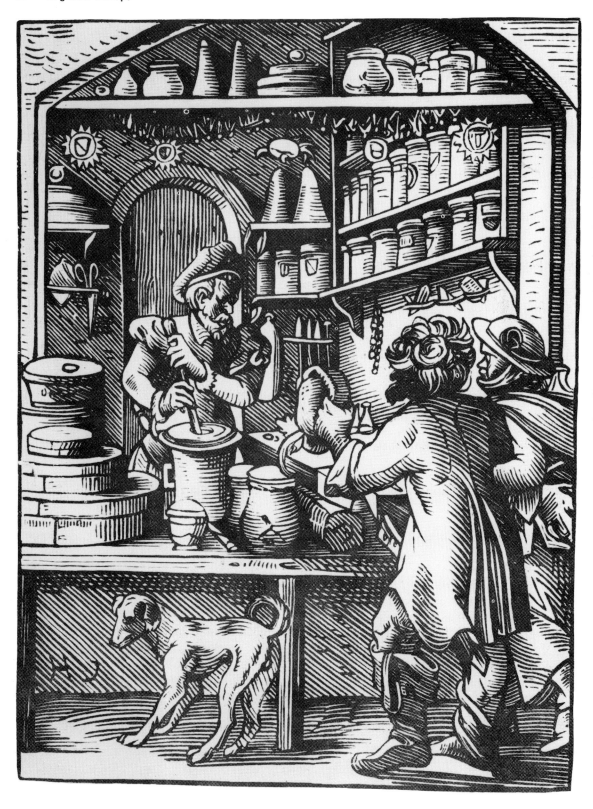

conditions, with many people forced to exist in one room. The luckier ones had small, thatched cottages.

Shops

All sorts of shops thrived in towns, many of them unfamiliar to us. There were cordwainers (cobblers), parchment makers, girdlers, fullers (laundrymen) and chandlers (candle-makers), as well as butchers, bakers and grocers. In London, and in other towns, whole streets were devoted to selling one kind of merchandise. For example, hosiers were found in Hosiery Lane and vintners (wine merchants) in Vintry Lane. Bread Street, Pudding Lane and the Poultry speak for themselves. West Cheap was the main London shopping area, but Goldsmith's Lane had the most expensive shops, and book buyers hurried to St Paul's churchyard. London Bridge was packed with shops and private houses. It was also the place where the heads of traitors were stuck on poles, serving as a grim warning to the passers-by.

Here are some typical prices the Elizabethans paid:

Pair of shoes	12d (5p)
Red cloak	20/- (£1)
2 rabbits	3d (1½p)
1 blanket	10/- (50p)
2 linen shirts	5/- (25p)
1 lb cheese	2d (1p)
1 brass kettle	22d (9p)

There was no paper money. The coins used were the gold sovereign worth £1, the

Paremptitius

d Anglos.

gold angel worth 10/-, gold and silver crowns worth 5/-, silver groats worth 4d, and shillings, sixpences and pennies.

Shops usually had only one room. The shutters could be pulled down to make jutting-out counters. There was often a workroom in the back which was shared by several craftsmen. Most shopkeepers belonged to guilds, which were similar to our trade unions. The guilds had strict rules, were well organized and made sure that the standard of their members' work and produce was high. Each guild had its own uniform, and its own patron saint — St Crispin was the patron saint of shoemakers, St Mark of saddlers and St Anthony of grocers.

Amenities

There were no county councils in Elizabthan times, and no rates to pay. Local government was carried out by Justices of the Peace. They provided some amenities, but not particularly efficiently. The Government ordered that local authorities should make sure that the streets were "made clean every day, saving Sunday", but this was rarely carried out. Townspeople were asked to "keep drainage channels against houses free from filth" but again, this was usually ignored. There was no reliable sewerage system, and most slops were emptied into the streets. Water was obtained by these methods:

spring and drinking water is enclosed in well sealed stone cisterns in different parts of the town; is let off through cocks into special wooden, iron bound vessels with broad bottoms and narrow tops, which poor labourers carry to and fro on their shoulders and sell.

There were also pumps and wells.

As for lighting, every citizen was meant to hang a lantern outside his house between

◄ **38** A water carrier.

Lanthorne and a whole Candell light. hange out your lights heare

39 A night-watchman.

six and nine o'clock at night if there was no moon. Night-watchmen called the hour throughout the night, for example:

12 o'clock, look well to your locks,
Your fire, your light and so goodnight.

A merchant's family

Merchants were prosperous and lived well in large, comfortable houses with their families, servants and apprentices. They could afford luxuries. For example, they might own glass from Venice, clocks from Germany, carpets from the East, as well as good-quality English ware. Merchant families enjoyed good food. Harrison (page 20) describes the sweet course of one meal:

. . . jellies of all colours, mixed with sundry flowers, herbs, trees, forms of beasts . . .

40 A cobbler's workshop. The master craftsman, right, supervising his apprentices.

and marchpanes wrought with no small curiosity; tarts of divers hues . . . conserves of old fruits, foreign and home-made; suckets [jams]; condinacs [quince-jellies]; marmalades, ginger-bread, florentines . . .

Children were brought up strictly and good manners were expected at all times. They got up at five or six o'clock in the morning, said their prayers and then helped their parents or went to school. At mealtimes, they served their parents first and had to wait politely and not leave the table until they had permission.

Apprentices

When they left school, many boys became apprentices. This meant that the boy went to live with a craftsman who taught him the skills of his trade. The master provided the apprentice with clothes, food, lodging and, of course, teaching. In return, the apprentice promised "not to absent himself from work, by night or day unlawfully". The Statute of Artificers 1563 stated that all apprentices had to train for a period of seven years. It also laid down the conditions of their apprenticeship, including the way they were to behave, and the wage they were to be paid. In 1588 an Act tried to stop the apprentices wearing flamboyant clothes and forbade them to wear bright colours or "locks of hair around their ears". In spite of all these rules, apprentices seem to have been a high-spirited group, often feuding and brawling in the streets. Girls occasionally became apprentices to learn skills such as glove-making.

44

41   A wedding feast, 1590, probably at the church of St Mary Magdalen, Bermondsey. In the background you can see the Tower of London. The artist has included some archers, musicians, and a man sitting in the stocks.

Amusements

There was always plenty to do and see in towns. In London boys practised archery in the Butts at Finsbury, or watched military musters at Mile End. Fleet Street was the place to go to see a "wonder". In 1581 a Dutch giant seven and a half feet tall and a three-foot-high dwarf were exhibited there to the delight of the crowd. At the Tower of London there "was kept a Menagerie containing three lionesses, a tiger, a lynx, a porcupine and an eagle". They were kept "in some remote place fitted up for the purpose with wooden lattices at the Queen's expence". St Paul's Cathedral was a popular place to go to meet friends, and was described as "a house of talking, or walking, or brawling, minstreling, of hawks and dogs". Not quite like the cathedral today! If this was not interesting enough, there were always the bear- and bull-baiting shows, or the theatre (see Chapter Nine).

Travel

No-one travelled for pleasure, for the roads were atrocious. By law, every labourer was ordered to work for six days a year on the roads in his area. Again, this was rarely

carried out. The most comfortable way to travel was on horseback. Girls rode side-saddle and had a special skirt which protected them from the mud. People travelled in small groups to protect themselves from highway robbers. Other less comfortable modes of travel included rickety carts and springless carriages. Rich families travelled through towns on litters, carried by two or four servants. Queen Elizabeth travelled in elaborate, but still very uncomfortable carriages. In London, the river Thames was used as a road and was always full of barges carrying either cargoes or sightseers.

Crimes

The dark, crowded streets were ideal haunts for cut-purses, thieves and pickpockets.

◄ 42 A lady rides side-saddle.

43 Queen Elizabeth in her carriage.
▼

44 Catholic priests, convicted of treason, are hung, drawn and quartered. This picture is from Foxe's *Book of Martyrs* (see picture 13).

Many of these criminals were children who had been carefully trained to steal by their parents, out of desperation or greed. If they were caught, they were put in the stocks where passers-by could torment them or throw things at them. Sometimes they had an ear cropped, or were branded with the letter "T" to warn the public. Liars were put in the pillory, and women who nagged too much were forced to wear a metal bridle. Hangings were frequent and drew large crowds. Crimes punishable by this method included highway robbery and poaching. Beheadings were a fairly common spectacle on Tower Green, but death by this method was reserved for the nobility. Traitors had to undergo the ghastly fate of being hung, drawn and quartered.

6 Poor Children

Who were the poor of Elizabethan England? Harrison defined them as "day labourers, poor husbandmen and some retailers which have no free land". He added proudly, but not entirely correctly that "as for slaves and bondsmen we have none". The number of poor increased enormously during the Elizabethan period. Harrison estimated that they numbered over ten thousand, but a modern historian believes that "grinding poverty was the lot of more than half the population".

The reasons for this increase were many.

45   A beggar.

46   A soap eater. These men ate soap to make themselves foam at the mouth so that people would think they suffered from the falling sickness and give them charity.

The rise in population, which meant that each family had more mouths to feed, expensive prices, high inflation and agrarian enclosures left many families unable to cope with the high cost of living. This was the case especially in the country: many farm labourers were forced to leave their homes and go to the towns in search of jobs, which often did not exist. Families had no choice but to beg or steal in order to stay alive. Vagabonds and beggars, as these homeless people were called, often grouped together into large bands, and the nursery rhyme "Hark, hark the dogs do bark, the beggars are coming to town" was about a frightening reality.

However, not all beggars were genuine unfortunates. Harrison believed that beggars could be divided into as many as twenty-five different categories, few of which were sincere. The Abraham Men, for example, pretended that they were mad, while the Counterfeit Cranks swallowed soap so that they would foam at the mouth — which was a symptom of the falling sickness. Others were rogues and tricksters who thrived on dishonest living and would not have accepted a job if it was offered to them. Such people forced their children to steal for them. Sometimes they deliberately maimed their children so that passers-by would feel sorry for them and give them money.

Obviously, infant mortality was very high amongst this group of children. The commonest causes of death were malnutrition, consumption and starvation, for parents could not afford to provide the food, clothes and shelter needed to keep them alive. Often parents became so desperate that they no longer cared what happened to their children and there are records in some church registers of nameless children found dead in the streets.

The Poor Laws

During the Elizabethan period people became aware that something had to be done to help the ever-increasing number of poor. Several important Acts were passed in 1563, 1572, 1576, 1597 and 1601 which tried, with a fair amount of success, to deal with the problem. These acts made it compulsory for local authorities to care for the "impotent, aged and needy" in their area. Money was collected for the poor by overseers or the priest in church on every Sunday and on Holy Days, and was evenly distributed amongst them. Poor children between the ages of five and fourteen were apprenticed to farmers and craftsmen who taught them a useful trade. The 1598 Act stated that this apprenticeship had to continue until girls were twenty-one, and boys twenty-four. Begging was strictly illegal.

Christ's Hospital

A few mediaeval hospices still existed in London which looked after poor children, orphans, the sick and travellers. St Bartholomew's cared for poor, sick people; Bethlehem looked after the insane; and poor children went to Christ's Hospital. Thomas Platter described the latter:

> I saw Christ's Hospital . . . which . . . finds food and clothes for seven hundred young boys and girls, while reading and writing are taught in a special school in the same, and they are kept here until they are fit for some craft or service . . . . They are all fine children taken from poor parents and put in here. They keep their hospital exceedingly clean. In the boys' long apartment are a hundred and forty beds in a row where they sleep two and two together and by their beds they have low chests in which to keep their clothes.

Christ's Hospital was so successful that it eventually developed into a famous public school.

The provinces

Other towns also attempted to help poor children. In Norwich, Ipswich, Bristol and Reading paupers were put into the care of

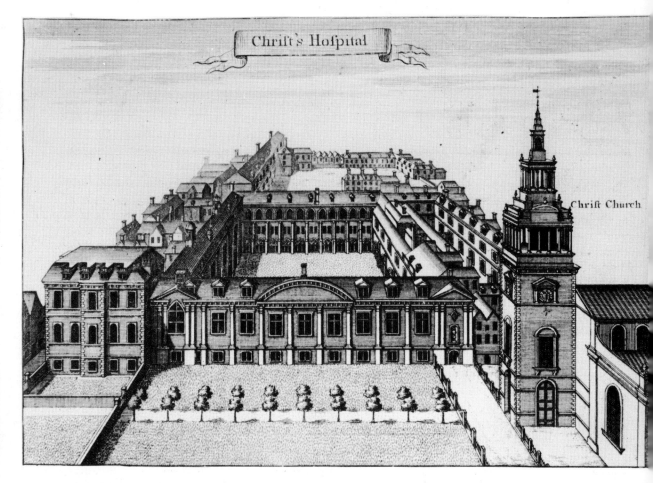

47 **Christ's Hospital where poor children in London were looked after.**

"select women" who taught them the basic skills. They also made the children do simple jobs for which they were given a small wage. Life was hard, for work began at 4.00 a.m. and continued until 7.00 p.m., with only a few breaks. Discipline was very strict and whipping was the usual punishment. However, the children were clothed and fed simply but adequately. The food ration for one day was: eight ounces of rye bread, a pint of porridge, a quarter pound of meat and one pint of beer.

Homes
Very poor people had no homes at all, but lived in fields or streets, or wherever they could find warmth and shelter. More fortunate families had a "mean, one roomed dwelling house, whence the whole family ate, slept and stored any possessions it might possess". Some had a little land on which they grew cabbages, parsnips and carrots but "as for wheaten bread, they eat it when they can reach onto the price of it, contenting themselves in the meantime with bread made of oats and barley".

7 Schools

The Elizabethans achieved a level of literacy and love of learning which was not attained again until the nineteenth century. Education was not compulsory and many people thought it unnecessary. One father declared disgustedly: "I would rather see my son hanged than a bookworm". But not everyone shared his view, and more and more people were thinking that education was a good thing. The Queen believed that education should be freely available to those who wanted it, and the number of schools grew during her reign. By 1575 there were three hundred and sixty grammar schools in existence. Some famous schools were founded in the Elizabethan period: Merchant Taylors (1561), Harrow (1590), Rugby (1567) and Uppingham (1584). Harrison wrote:

> there are not many corporate towns now under the Queen's dominion that have not one grammar school at least, with sufficient living for a master and an usher, appointed to the same.

The first educational book of any standard was written at this time by Roger Ascham, tutor to Lady Jane Grey and the Queen. It was called the *Scholemaster* and contained many modern ideas, including the belief that children learnt nothing from beatings, but much from observation and discovery.

Grammar schools

Grammar schools varied enormously. Some were so small that there was only one room, one master and a handful of pupils. Others had at least one hundred children and several masters and ushers (assistants). Parents had to pay a termly fee, but if they were too poor to be able to afford it, their son had his education free in return for doing odd jobs around the school.

Boys went to grammar school when they were seven years old. They were expected to work hard, and if they failed to come up to standard they were dismissed, for there were always plenty of other boys eager for the place. At Eton, one of the rules was: "if there be any dullard, the master giveth his friends warning and putteth him away, that he faileth not at shcool". A school day was long and arduous, beginning at 7.00 a.m. and finishing at 5.00 p.m. There was a two-hour break for lunch. Boys were expected to be polite and courteous at all times, as well as hard-working. Pupils went to school every day except Sunday. There were a few holidays — twelve days at Christmas and Easter, and the odd day here and there, such as Shrove Tuesday.

The curriculum

Latin was the main subject, and children were encouraged to speak it at all times. Greek and sometimes Hebrew were taught as second and third languages. Divinity was another important subject and boys had to learn the Commandments, Articles of Faith and long extracts from the Bible. Rhetoric (the art of public speaking) and logic (clear thinking and the art of arguing) were also considered valuable, as were arithmetic, geometry and astronomy. If parents were

willing to pay a little extra, pupils also had singing and dancing lessons. There were no special periods for P.E. or games, but sometimes the master let the boys play draughts or practise archery.

Equipment

Because paper was so expensive, boys were expected to learn most things off by heart rather than write things down. Every schoolboy needed a Bible, a Latin grammar, ink, quills, various textbooks and a satchel to carry them all in. This equipment cost about £13 2s 6d. Boys wrote on slates or on writing tablets made out of soft wax held in a wooden frame. The main textbooks included William Lily's *Standard Latin Grammar*, Nicholas Udall's *Flower of Latin Speaking* and a collection of *Vulgaria* — books written in the vulgar tongue of English.

Masters

Most schoolmasters were graduates and all were clerics, because of the importance laid on religious education. After 1544 all masters had to have a licence obtained from a Bishop. A master's salary was very low.

48   A small class in Stratford Grammar School.

49   A modern photograph of Stratford Grammar School.

The average pay was just over £13 a year and so teaching did not attract the most learned of men. As there was no retiring age a master could go on forever. Hugh Rhodes stressed the importance of having suitable men as masters and said:

> if ye put them [children] to school, see that their masters be such as fear God and live virtuously, such as can punish sharply with patience and not with vigour, for it doth oft make them rebel and run away.

As at home, discipline was very strict. One poor boy complained: "my master hath beat my back and side while the rod would hold to his hand". Another moaned that his master beat him merely to keep himself warm! Here is a description of a "good" teacher:

> in the morning he [the master] would exactly and plainly construe and parse the lesson to his scholar; which done he slept his hour . . . in his desk in the

school; but woe to any scholar that slept the while. Awaking, he heard them accurately . . . it may be said that others have taught as much learning with fewer lashes. Yet his sharpness was the better endured, because unpartial and many excellent scholars were bred under him.

Early education — rich children
Most noble and gentry families employed one or more tutors to teach their children at home as soon as they were considered able enough. This was often at as young an age as three or four. Boys were tutored at home until they were seven when they either went to grammar school or became pages (see page 35). Tutors sometimes stayed on in the family to teach the daughters, who received as good, if not better education than their brothers. They learnt the Classics, modern studies such as French and literature, science and lighter subjects like music and dancing. They were also allowed to go hunting, hawking, fishing and to practise archery.

Early education — country children
If their parents wanted, most country children were able to have an education. Endowed schools were run by "poor women or others whose necessities compel them to undertake it as a mere shelter from begging". These were the equivalent of the nineteenth-century dame schools and the standard cannot have been high. Other schools were

50 A page from a Greek grammar book, written in Latin, from Westminster School, London, 1598.

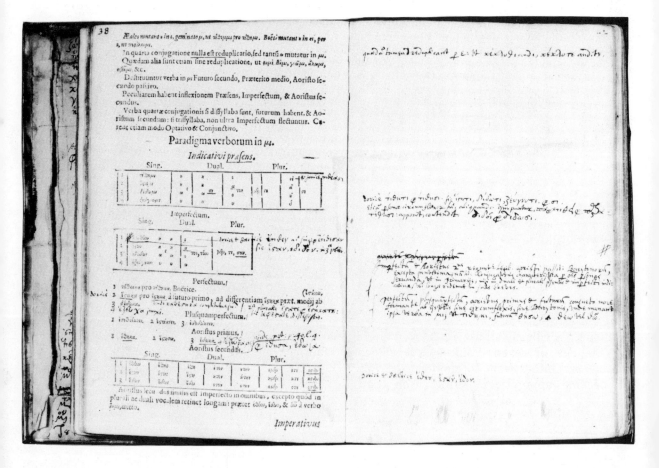

set up by priests or church-wardens who taught very young children. There were petty schools which were similar to our primary schools. Here children learnt to read and write and to recite parts of the Bible. Sometimes horn books were available. A horn book consisted of one printed page mounted on wood, covered with a transparent layer of animal horn which was fastened with strips of metal. Horn books contained spellings, alphabets and prayers. At the age of seven children left village schools and either went to grammar schools or became apprentices. More often than not boys stayed at home to help their fathers.

51   On the left a boy is beaten, while the master on the right has his rod ready for anyone who misbehaves. On the left-hand side one pupil is holding a horn book.

Private schools

There were a small number of private schools in existence. Many of them had been founded by Huguenot refugees, or else they were run by private individuals. They offered the same curriculum as grammar schools, but also taught modern subjects such as French and English history. Private schools were open to boys between the ages of five and seventeen, and occasionally took boarders.

8 The Universities and the Inns of Court

During the reign of Edward VI (1547-1553) Latimer, a former bishop of Worcester, had complained that "the Universities do wondrously decay already", but under Elizabeth I they enjoyed a revival. There were considered to be three Universities — Oxford, Cambridge and the Inns of Court in London. A small number of wealthy Elizabethan boys could complete their education at one of these three institutions.

Students

Almost anyone who could afford it could go to University when he left school. (As usual, girls were not even considered.)

52 The dining hall in Middle Temple Hall, one of the Inns of Court. The law students who dined here were probably more well-behaved than the Oxford and Cambridge students who dined in similar halls at their universities. One of the tables in this hall in London is made from the wooden timbers of Sir Francis Drake's ship, the *Golden Hind*.

53 Lincoln's Inns.

Students did not need to have passed particular exams, nor did they have to be particularly intelligent. But they did have to be able to prove that they could read and write reasonably well in Latin and, above all, they had to be wealthy enough to stay at University.

The average age for going up to University was younger than it is today. Most boys were fifteen or sixteen when they started, but some were as young as twelve or thirteen. They usually went to the college their father had been to, or to one that had been recommended by a close friend. The Master's degree course took seven years (the same as an apprenticeship), but most boys were content to do the four-year Bachelor's degree course. Some boys only went to University for a year or so, just to say that they had been!

University life

Rooms were usually provided for a student in the college or in the town. Most lodgings were pretty basic and students had to provide their own furnishings and means of heating. A room in Oxford in the 1590s cost £1 a year, while a smaller one cost ten shillings. At Cambridge, students had to pay £20 a year for all their living expenses.

Food was provided, but it was not very good and consisted of a monotonous diet of "boiled beef and pottage, bread and beer . . . and no more". Some tried to smuggle in extra goodies but, officially, this was not allowed. Students had to abide by many rules. They were not allowed to wear luxurious clothes, have long hair, keep dogs, visit alehouses, play cards or stay out later than nine o'clock at night. In spite of these restrictions, students were still able to enjoy themselves. One Elizabethan complained that "they ruffle and roist it out . . . exceeding in apparel and ranting riotous company". Another described a typical mealtime scene:

> The [students] had to be restrained from dining in their hats and from scrambling for their food at the dresser in the Hall. Occasionally they came to fisticuffs and the Hall furniture generally required mending after revels.

Curriculum

Students could start the course at any time, but they had to complete sixteen full terms before they qualified as a Bachelor. The day began at 5.00 a.m. and continued until 6.00 p.m., depending how conscientious each student was. Teaching was through lectures and tutorials, the students being fined if they did not attend. Mostly, it depended upon the individual as to how much work was done.

The subjects the Elizabethan students had to learn seem stuffy and restricted compared with the hundreds of subjects offered today. The Elizabethan curriculum was based on the Trivium (grammar, logic and rhetoric) and the Quadrivium (geometry, arithmetic, astronomy and music). Latin was the favourite language for speaking, teaching and learning, although Greek was also considered necessary. A few "modern" subjects like French, Italian, geography and history, were slowly becoming acceptable. At the end of the course there was no exam, but each student had to give a "disputation" in front of his tutors and fellow students. One student proposed a motion for debate, and another opposed it. Marks were given according to how well they argued.

Religious teaching was not neglected and students were expected to go to church at least twice on Sundays, as well as to say regular prayers, both in public and privately.

The Inns of Court

There were four Inns of Court for training lawyers: Greys Inn, which had two hundred and twenty fellows; Middle Temple which had one hundred and ninety; Inner Temple which had one hundred and eighty-nine; and Lincoln's Inn which had one hundred and sixty. There were also nine Courts of Chancery which offered pupils a preparatory year before they went on to the main Inns.

The average age of admission into the Inns was thirteen or fourteen. The course lasted seven years, and on qualifying the fellow was known as an Utter Barrister. After another five years' training he was allowed into the real, practising law courts, but to be considered experienced he had to do at least another ten years.

The training given at the Inns was based on the history of Law; reasoning; logic; practical argument and French, which was the language of the Courts. Fellows attended court cases very regularly. There was no fee for tuition, but fellows had to find their own board and lodgings. Life in the Inns was very similar to that at Oxford and Cambridge, except that budding lawyers seem to have been more responsible, in spite of the attractions of London. The historian G. M. Young believes that the Inns provided "the liveliest, most intelligent and certainly the most influential society England could furnish".

54   Oak doors at Middle Temple Hall. Although the law students were more responsible than the Oxford and Cambridge ones, there were some heavy drinking celebrations one Christmas, and as a result these doors with their spiked tops were put in and kept locked over the Christmas period from then on.

9 Games and Pastimes

The Queen loved lavish entertainment and encouraged her subjects to do the same. She liked to go on Royal Progresses throughout the land, visiting noble families. At their homes she expected to be fed and amused as befitted her queenly status — which often left the family in huge debt. On a less royal level, ordinary people entered into games and pastimes full of enthusiasm and vigour. The restrictive clothes the children wore do not seem to have stopped them from enjoying themselves.

Football and outdoor sports

We would not recognize the Elizabethan's version of football and our own version by comparison is very tame indeed. Every Shrove Tuesday country people held inter-village football matches on the village common or in the main street. The ball was placed in the centre of the field and the two teams lined up at opposite ends, ready to thunder towards each other in an attempt to get the ball first. There were few rules, the simple objective being to get as many goals as possible. A horrifying amount of violence took place: ". . . sometimes their necks are broken, sometimes their backs . . . sometimes their noses gush out blood".

Another popular outdoor sport was cudgels. The object of this game was to form pairs and then try to knock each other out with wooden cudgels! Less violent, but equally energetic games included running, jumping, fencing, jousting, archery and skittles. Fishing seems to have been the most relaxing and harmless pastime.

Hunting and hawking

In the country fox-hunting was considered a social duty — and was enthusiastically carried out. Stag, roe and buck were also hunted, as were badgers, otters, hares and boars. Hounds were especially bred for the purpose and Harrison proudly informs us that "there is no country [to] compare with ours in number, excellency and diversity of our dogs". Hawking was a gentleman's sport, not considered suitable for yeomen. The hawks for hunting were as carefully trained and pampered as the hounds. Stubbes, a Puritan, pointed out that "some people spend more in a year on hawks and hounds than they would give to the poor in seven".

Indoor games

Card games were much enjoyed, the favourite being Triumph (the same as our Whist). Chess, dice, backgammon and draughts were played on cold winter evenings, while children entertained themselves with leap-frog, blind-man's-buff and hide-and-seek.

Music and dancing

All Elizabethans seem to have been extremely musical. Children were encouraged to learn to sing and dance at a very early age and it was usual for a family to sit down with their servants to enjoy a musical evening together. There was a large choice of musical instruments to play. For example, keyboard instruments like the harpsichord, clavichord, dulcimer and virginals were very popular; woodwind included recorders and crumhorns; and in the string section were lutes and rebecs. As for songs, the most enjoyed were madrigals in which several voices sang different melodies at the same time.

The range of dances was considerable too. There was the solemn and dignified pavanne or the lively galliard, and others had lovely, imaginative names like Farnaby's Woodycock, Nobody's Jig and Shake a Trot.

Theatres

Interest in the theatre grew, encouraged by the works of our most famous playwright William Shakespeare. Theatres sprang up all over London and in the provinces, and included the famous Globe, the Swan and the Fortune, which was built in 1600 for £400. Thomas Platter tells how

> daily at two in the afternoon, London has two, sometimes three plays running in different places . . . . The playhouses are so construed that they [the actors]

are on a raised platform so that everyone has a good view. . . . Whoever cares to stand below pays one penny, but if he wishes to sit he enters by another door and pays another penny . . . . During the performance food and drinks are carried around the audience.

As there was no electricity, performances were always given in the daytime. There was little scenery but props could be disgustingly realistic — in death scenes guts and hearts were strewn across the stage, freshly bought from the local butcher! All actors were male, for it was not considered decent for women to show themselves on stage. The behaviour of the audience in the playhouses was described:

> in our assemblies at plays in London, you shall see such heaving and shoving, such itching and shouldering to sit by women, such care for their garments that they not be trod upon . . . such pillows to their backs, that they take no hurt . . . such tickling, such toying, such smiling, such winking.

Bull- and bear-baiting

Not all Elizabethan entertainments were as

55   Fishing, one of the quieter Elizabethan pastimes.

▼

56   An illustration from *The Book of Faulconrie* or *Hawking for the onely delight and pleasure of all Noblemen and Gentlemen*, 1575

▼

57   The marriage feast of Sir Henry Unton. There ➤ is music to accompany the meal.

pleasant as the theatre. Today we would consider the baiting of defenceless animals unnecessarily cruel, but we must remember that the Elizabethans lived in more brutal, desperate times than we do. Thomas Platter described what happened:

> every Sunday and Wednesday in London there are bear baitings . . . . The theatre is circular with galleries around the top for spectators . . . . In the middle of this place a large bear on a rope was bound to a stake, then a number of great English mastiffs were brought in and shown first to the bear which afterwards they baited, one after the other . . . although they were much struck and mauled by the bear, they did not give in . . . . The bear's teeth were not sharp so they could not injure the dogs.

The new fashion of smoking was becoming popular, as one spectator noticed: "at bear baitings and everywhere else, the English are constantly smoking the Nicotinian Weed".

58   Country people dancing to a drum.

Cock-fighting

This was another barbarous yet popular sport.

> In the City of London . . . cock fightings are held annually throughout three quarters of the year . . . and I saw the place which is built like a theatre. In the centre . . . stands a circular table covered with straw . . . where the cocks are teased and incited to fly at one and another . . . . I am told that the stakes on a cock often amount to thousands of pounds.

The most famous cockpit in London was at Drury Lane but most towns and villages had their own pits. On Shrove Tuesday schoolboys were allowed to bring fighting cocks to school and the entire afternoon was spent in putting bets on their favourite cocks.

Holy-days

There had been over ninety holy-days before the Reformation, but there were only twenty-seven by Elizabeth's reign. Although a few people frowned on this celebration of saints' days, most families loved and looked forward to them. Everyone had a day off work or school, and the time was spent in drinking, playing or going to fairs. The main holy-days were Shrove Tuesday, Mothering Sunday, Plough Monday and the twelve days of Christmas. At Whitsun a huge flagon of ale was passed round the church and everyone in the congregation was offered a sip. This ceremony was called the Church-Ale and was much enjoyed.

59   The Globe Theatre.

10 Health and Medicine

As we have already seen, Elizabethan families, with their poor amenities, were not too concerned about things which today are considered essential for a healthy, hygienic life. The towns, filthy and over-crowded, were ideal places for germs to breed and spread. Little attention was paid to personal cleanliness and nobody worried if their children failed to clean their teeth regularly or wash behind their ears. The solution to body smells and dirt was to apply more perfume or more make-up. It did not occur to people that regular washing might help. Queen Elizabeth prided herself on having a bath once a month, but few of her subjects followed her example. Laundry was done once every two or three months. Elizabethan mothers had to take their dirty washing to the nearest stream, or else pound it in great wooden tubs.

Disease and death were therefore common and accepted as part of everyday life. There were doctors, but few of them were as trustworthy as this one:

A worthy physician is the enemy of sickness . . . his action is most in feeling of pulses, and his discourse chiefly of the nature of the disease . . . . He persuades abstinence and patience for the benefit of health, while purging and bleeding are the chief courses of his counsel.

Hospitals were mostly unpleasant and inadequate, with brutal, untrained nurses and four to six patients in one bed.

Elizabethans still had a very mediaeval attitude towards medicine. They believed that the body was made up of four humours, or fluids — blood, phlegm, melancholy and bile. A person's personality depended upon which fluid he had most of in his body: the personality was either sanguine (red-haired and lusty); or phlegmatic (weak and cool); or melancholic (brooding and morbid); or bilious (hot-tempered, sallow complexion). It was best to have a balance of all four, for an excess of any one could lead to an illness. Imbalance of the humours was prevented by herbs, diet, astrology, charms and purging the blood. As we shall see, some of these "cures" were rather bizarre, based on superstition rather than knowledge.

Children

All children were born phlegmatic. Therefore, they were fed on cool, moist foods such as milk, cheese and white meats like chicken. At the age of thirteen they were allowed to go on to "grosser meats, and wine mixed with water". Old people were also thought to be phlegmatic and were fed on the same food as children.

Herbs

As well as being used extensively in cooking, herbs were believed to have healing properties and were used to sooth hundreds of complaints. For example, cowslips were taken to ease madness, violets for tertian ague, raspberry leaf by women in labour, comfrey for bronchitis, mint for digestion, fennel for liver complaints and camomile for insomnia. Herbs were useful in combating the plague:

In such infectious times it is good for

every man . . . to use [herbs] daily, specially in the morning and evening, to burn Juniper, or Rosemary, or Bay leaves or Marjoram or Frankincense.

Astrologers

Astrologers and wise women were consulted regularly for advice on how to treat certain diseases. Illnesses were sometimes attributed to evil spirits, witches or spiteful neighbours, and many an old woman was unjustly accused of acts she could not possibly have performed. Amulets and charms were worn to protect against demons and illness. Garnets worn round the neck prevented melancholy, and emeralds calmed the mind. Remember how babies were given coral necklaces as presents (page 10).

Cures

Bleeding and purging (draining the blood) were popular cures, for it was believed that as the blood flowed out, so would the illness. Other cures were semi-magical and relied on some peculiar ingredients. Donkey skin worn

▲
60   Doctors

61   On the right an infusion of Guaiacum bark is prepared. On the left the doctor gives it to his patient. This wood was believed to cure syphilis, gout, stones and other diseases.
▼

around the neck helped rheumatism. People suffering from gout were recommended to boil a red-haired dog alive in oil until it fell apart, then add worms, hog's marrow and herbs and apply the mixture to the affected parts. For deafness:

> put nothing on to the ear except it be as warm as blood. Then take the gall of an hare and mix it with the grease of a fox and with blade will instil it into the ear . . . or else take the juice of worm wood and temper it with the gall of bull and . . . put it into the ear.

For baldness:

> shave the head and beard and anoint the head with the grease of a fox . . . or else wash the head with the juice of beetles four or five times or else stamp garlic and rub the head with it and after that wash it with vinegar.

The recipes do not mention how the ingredients were obtained.

Plague and smallpox

The main diseases which the Elizabethans suffered from were syphilis, sweating sickness, smallpox, scarlet fever, gout, asthma, consumption and plague. The plague was highly contagious and quick to strike. This is what happened:

> When the plague is in . . . a country . . . houses, the which be infected in town or city, be closed up both doors and windows, and the inhabitants shall not come abroad neither to church, nor to market nor to any other house for infecting other the which be clean of infection . . . . I have known it when the straw and rushes have been cast out of a house infected the hogs which did lie in it, died of the pestilence.

There was no cure for plague, but rue was put on window-sills in a vain attempt to keep it at bay. In 1594 a Pest House was built in St Giles, Cripplegate, but it was unable to cope with the number of people infected.

Smallpox was less dangerous, especially for children, and so parents put their children near infected cases, so that they would get the disease over with while they were still young. (The attitude today towards German measles is much the same.) People suffering from smallpox had red curtains hung round their beds and at the windows, for the sun's rays filtering through red were thought to be beneficial.

Apothecaries

These were men who sold everything from herbs to the most deadly of poisons. Shakespeare gives a lively description of one:

> *And in his needy shop a tortois hung*
> *An alligator stuffed and other skins*
> *Of ill-shaped fishes, and about his shelves*
> *A beggarly account of empty boxes*
> *Green earthen pots, bladders and musty*
> *seeds,*
> *Remnants of packthread and old cakes*
> *of roses*
> *Were thinly scattered to make up a show.*

Death

Death was never far away and few Elizabethans lived to what we would consider old age. It was believed that people were born as the tide came in, and died as the tide went out. When death came near, all the doors and windows of the house were opened so that the spirit could go out unhindered. Bells were solemnly rung, and the body was wrapped in a shroud — if it was a baby, his Chrism clothes were used instead. Very young babies were buried with little cere-

62   **A devil carrying a witch to hell.**

mony or sadness, but infants were given a lavish funeral and were sadly missed. Black clothes were worn by the family, and black drapes were hung in the dead person's room. The coffins of children and unmarried girls were accompanied by children dressed in white, and over the coffin was put a white cloth to denote the innocence of the dead child. Sometimes, as in 1603:

the streets [were] strewn with flowers when maids of any sort [were] buried . . .

as for bachelors, they [wore] Rosemary. If a young girl died the place where she used to sit in church was decorated with a Maiden's Garland.

It was popular to be buried inside the church, with a plaque, brass or memorial erected in memory, but unbaptized babies and suicides were buried in the northern end of the churchyard.

63   The sickbed of Sir Henry Unton.

64 The funeral of Queen Elizabeth, 28 April 1603. Her coffin is followed by 2) the Kings at Arms, 3) noblemen, 4) the Archbishop of Canterbury, 5) the French Ambassador and his train-bearer, 6) the Earl of Pembroke with the Standard of England, 7) the Master of the Horse, 8) the Lady Marchioness of Northampton, grand mourner, and the ladies in attendance on the Queen, 9) the Captains of the Guard, 10) Lord Clanricarde with the standard of Ireland, 11) Viscount Bindon with the standard of Wales, followed by the Lord Mayor, 12) Gentlemen of the Chapels Royal and Children of the Chapels Royal, 13) trumpeters, 14) Standard of the Lion, 15) Standard of the Greyhound, 16) the Queen's horse, 17) poor women, to the number of 266, 18) the Banner of Cornwall, the aldermen, recorders, town clerks, etc. There was a strict order for the mourners, as there was for the classes of society.

Date List

1558	Elizabeth I came to the throne
	Elizabethan Church Settlement
1559	Treaty of Château Cambresis, and expulsion of Huguenots from France
1561	Mary Queen of Scots leaves France and returns to Scotland
1563	Statute of Artificers
1567	Rugby School founded
1569	Rising of the Northern Earls
1570	Elizabeth excommunicated by the Pope
	Growth of Puritanism
	Ridolfi Plot
1571	Jesus College, Oxford founded
1572	Massacre of the Huguenots on St Bartholomew's Day
1574	Arrival of first Jesuit missionaries
1575	William Byrd receives a monopoly for printed music
1577	Sir Francis Drake circumnavigates the world
1578	Development of the Navy under Hawkins
1580	Jesuit mission directed by Edmund Campion
1584	Emmanuel College, Cambridge founded
	Throckmorton Plot
1585	Start of war with Spain
1587	Drake singes the King of Spain's beard
	Death of Mary Queen of Scots
1588	Defeat of the Spanish Armada
1593	Shakespeare writes his first play *Love's Labour's Lost*
1595	Hardwick Hall built
	The Ulster Rebellion
1596	Death of Sir Francis Drake
1597	Sir John Harrington invents the first water closet
	The most important of all the Poor Relief Acts is passed
1599	East India Company founded
	The Earl of Essex's expedition to Ireland
1603	Death of Elizabeth I, and accession of James I

Glossary

agrarian enclosures	village land which was enclosed (hedged) to make way for pasture
apprenticeship	seven-year period during which the apprentice learned a craft or trade
chandler	candle-maker; or someone who sold provisions for ships
changeling	fairy child, which might be swapped with a newly born baby
Chrism clothes	the special clothes a newly baptized baby was dressed in to show that it had become a Christian
cordwainer	shoemaker
Courts of Chancery	the nine lesser Inns of Court
disputation	scholarly argument, which was used as a type of exam
endowed schools	schools which were set up by private patrons, and received an annual sum of money to help them
gentry	well-born country people
guilds	organizations which protected various crafts and trades
houses of easement	Elizabethan lavatories
labourer	man who hired himself out to work on a farm
Lord of Misrule	man who was chosen to lead the festivities at Christmas
logic	the art of reasoning
marchpane	the Elizabethan name for marzipan
knot garden	formal garden, where the shrubs were laid out in knot-shaped patterns
nobility	high-born people, often related to the royal family
pargeting	moulded plasterwork on the outside walls of houses
pomander	sweet-smelling sachet or ball made from herbs or dried oranges stuck with cloves, which was held to the nose to block out unpleasant smells
Quadrivium	four of the main subjects learned at University — geometry, arithmetic, astronomy and music
rhetoric	the art of public speaking
Rocking Cake	cake baked for the father at the christening of his child
scavenger	a type of Elizabethan dustman
tenant farmer	man who rented and then farmed land
Trivium	the three main subjects learned at grammar school and at the Universities — grammar, logic and rhetoric
usher	assistant teacher
vagabond	unemployed person who wandered from town to town
wise woman	woman who could foretell the future and practise good magic
yeoman	well-off farmer who owned his own land

Places to Visit

Hardwick Hall, Derbyshire (home of the famous Bess of Hardwick)
Longleat House, Wiltshire
Burghley House, Northamptonshire
Middle Temple Hall (famous for its marvellous roof)
Lord Leycester's Hospital, Warwick (an ancient guild, restored in Elizabethan times by Elizabeth's favourite)
Mary Arden's house, Warwickshire (decorated in much the same way as it would have been in Elizabeth's time. Home of Shakespeare's mother)
Stratford Grammar School (a good example of an Elizabethan grammar school)
Little Moreton Hall, Cheshire (the ultimate in black and white timber framing)
National Portrait Gallery (for many miniatures dating from this period)
Victoria and Albert Museum (for clothes and household articles dating from Elizabethan times)
The London Museum, Barbican (for everyday things)
British Museum (for old woodcuts and engravings from the period)

Books for Further Reading

Non-fiction
Burton, E., *The Elizabethans at Home*, Secker and Warburg, 1958
Dodd, A.H., *Life in Elizabethan England*, Batsford, 1961
Harrison and Royston, *How They Lived*, Blackwell, 1963
Hole, C., *English Home Life*, Batsford, 1947
Holme, M., *Elizabethan London*, Cassell, 1969
Quennell, *A History of Everyday Things*, Batsford, 1901
Shakespeare's England

Index

The numbers in **bold type** refer to the figure numbers of the illustrations